LIMERENCE

Exploring Infatuation

an anthology of poetry and prose
by Ashleigh Abul

External cover by Ashleigh Abul.

ISBN: 978-1723466779

Contents

LIMERENCE

To my Mum -
who I'm sure
infused her love of creativity
into me while I was cocooned in her
womb;

To Ducky -
my true albeit taller younger
sister,
who encouraged me to grow,
helped me find and accept my voice;

To Dan -
who listened as I transformed
thoughts into poetry,
editing ears open,
ever patient;

And finally,

To Cat -
who remains oblivious
of the fact
that without her,
none of these poems
would have ever
entered existence.

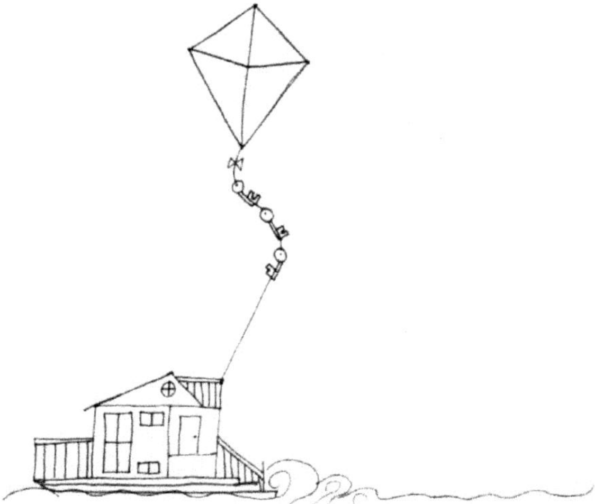

Spark (and so it begins).

Are lightning strikes contagious
or simply agents of fate?
My mind is
enticed,
enchanted,
charmed -
tumultuously oscillating,
ascending toward clouds;
dark, monochrome shades
reminiscent of black hellebore.

I am tied to my ship,
a cognitive kite with cauda of keys,
soaring to new heights,
string taut above the sea;
rebelling against the imminent
plight,
it resonates in the gale.

Flash!
A current disseminates;
sky to kite, ship to shore.
And I am
a live wire,
inspired,
struck -
no casualties
except
a causation,
a realization,
a calling;

it's you.

Morning routine.

8 am -
I wake, late,
after turbulent sleep.
Welcome intruder,
please,
stop dream walking.
You enkindle homesickness -
How?
I've never belonged anywhere.

Focus;
reign in the bedlam,
brain still slightly numb;
vivid visions vanish,
slip away,
phosphenes fade from my eyes,
yet my thoughts inevitably
return to you.

I tumble into consciousness,
with the ritual, habitual
turning of taps;
water scalds.
Please,
cleanse me.
Rather, a rain of ice shards
startles, shocks my skin.
I have always pushed my luck.

But how I relish
running my hands through coloured
cloth,
melanin, just another shade of
rainbow;
no melancholy appearances allowed.
Which enigma,
end of the spectrum,
shall I embody today?

Porridge and 6 emails for breakfast,
notebook nearby, naturally,
how comforting.
Next,
the first of four loads of washing,
floral bubbles,
scented steam;
fresh bed sheets tonight.
How fragrant this hour of the
morning is.

In the interim,
time is currency -
I tune,
creating an even tone,
wood vibrating against my
collarbone,
absolute control throughout my bow;
there will be no disorder here.

Let the music strip back my brain,
turpentine,
timbre creating clarity,

serpentine patterns of thought
amongst the chaos.
Only now do I feel clean,
raw.

And so
the day has begun -
the usual routine refusal,
the same quiet, covert confusion,
or simply,
just the typical ways
of avoiding my feelings for you.

Four seconds of common sense.

Careful, dear heart.
Don't start -
don't get carried away.

Capitulation.

Destination unknown,
objective unclear;
let me run
      hellbent
            after you
                  nevertheless.

Utopia.

Dear sanctuary,
brilliant horizon,
beacon of hope -
you beckon my boat,
compass cracked, broken;
      the Kraken,
            now my comrade;
I am no longer lost,
hurtling haphazardly,
hurling through
      this hurricane
                  no more.

So -
please remain
blissfully oblivious.
I will
      tame these tides,
explore realms unknown,
steer, steadfast,
      against the rain
            until I reach
                  your shore.

Cardiac hypoxia.

This calescent, crowded room
between us;
alternatively -
our shared existence
in the same space,
every nuance of your presence
obliterating the physics of
sound,
      distance,
              time;
my heart,
hypnotised,
      haemostatic,
              hungry to be heard
through layers of white noise.

On your chatoyance.

I hereby enclose my heart,
atria, aorta and all,
resting beneath my clavicle,
crystalline, cognizant,
concupiscent,
it transparently reveals
my fondness for you,
blood gushing, rushing,
ventricles full,
as superluminal optic journeys take
flight;
I catch your eye.

And how I long for your gaze -
pale, pearlescent, nacreous sea
glass,
glancing at me
intermittently,
intelligent, iridescent
in dark painted, palpebral frames.
Do you know in your line of sight,
lingering looks,
I feel
deliciously limpid,
lucid,
ludicrous?

I refrain from being lackadaisical,
feel such an intense sensation,
avert, escape your x-ray vision,
trembling,

tingling,
my heart turbulent
at the touch of your eyes,
your words,
tangible
regardless of the time and space
between us.

And yet,
there is a narcotic, nebulous
quality
in our conversations;
so I still haven't discerned
whether your eyes are green or blue.
But what eloquence lies
beneath your enigma,
what capricious
            comedy and
                  cleverness.

Entity.

You are a cosmos,
a cynosure,
every millisecond of bliss an
eternity,
always gone too soon.

Subtext.

"Do you have a lover?"

No.

(Would you let me sense a new
tactile nucleus,
focus on every millimetre of your
hand,
the warmth of your skin,
the electricity of your touch?
Such voltage surges through my
veins,
conducted by our contact,
setting my heart aflame,
a beacon, ablaze,
an uncontrollable inferno.

Intricate glass is forged in fire;
passion, fervour, ardour.
Refractions from my crystal
admiration
illuminate my irides
as I adore you,
await your acknowledgement;
a return trip,
drive me crazy forever,
please let me be your passenger
again -
always.)

Post office ingénue.

So I send you my heart;
a gift.
Take it if you dare,
prepare,
for I will bravely throw caution
and logic to the wind.
But -
if my affections are an affliction,
if you consider my heart a
hinderance,
cannot ever love me,
if the juxtaposition of stage
lights, tall children and the music
of your creation, inspiration,
incited hallucinations,
tell me
before I relinquish my dignity.

Please return my brain,
now a fleshy, pulpy, clump of
visceral entropy,
send back my heart,
reply paid,
so I can cauterize its candour,
decontaminate and disinfect its
diathesis.
forgive me,
for I am foolish, young,
enamoured and awed by your
experience,
and cannot help but love you.

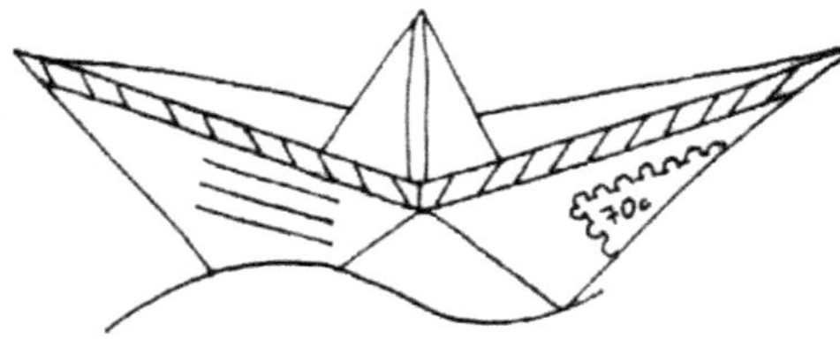
70c

Unrequited.

You are enough
to rock any captain's boat;
no longer orientated by the stars
but by the ripples your kind heart
offers her ship.

However -
We do not sail upon the same waters,
my love is no anchor.
Pursue no nonexistent lighthouse,
expect no heart to fall in your
hands,
be not surprised when you reel in,
hook returned

empty.

Fool.

Amateur sleuth,
restless until resolution;
regrettable -
I reflect and reminisce,
but renounce my proclivities,
refuse to shriek
"eureka!"
for an answer,
in retrospect,
not unexpected,
yet disappointing
nonetheless.

I am discouraged,
albeit reluctantly,
disenchanted,
disillusioned all the same.
My heart is
inevitably
no longer in denial;
in limerence no more.

Eighteen years
is a gully too wide,
a river too deep
to wade across.
Drowning is a fascinating,
spellbinding,
hypnotic prospect.

But

I would rather
watch the water
wash away my disappointment,
just another memory,
a flimsy, pathetic paper boat,
sailing under life's bridge,
slow inundation, deluge,
easily dragged under a torrent of
new experiences.

Why then,
heart,
must you persist,
resist the imminent cloudburst,
flash flood,
longing to jump,
plunge,
reckless,
off your own waterfall
into her ravine -
no prospect of survival?

Lunacy.

And although
you are my moon,
pale and dazzling
upon the distant horizon,
I silently watch
as you leave
with the tide.

I know
I can only touch
the light of your reflection
upon my water in moments fleeting,
that you will never stay for long,
that I will never
get close enough
to feel your gentle warmth
radiate through my bones.

I know
my secret adoration for you is
unrequited,
impossible.
But,
that's okay.

I am a clandestine soul,
content
to simply bask
in your light.
After all,

that's enough
to keep
my candle burning
day and night.

Heart's decay.

Soon
you will transcend time,
destined to succumb to
eventual evanescence,
just a memory,
just another person I let my heart
long for in vain.
My desires are all translucence;
stay.

Please don't fade,
grow lethargic, listless,
linger in my mind,
insubstantial,
blurry shades of torpor, narcosis,
my fondness for you
failing, feeble,
diminishing, dulling,
like cold hands,
numb, no longer feeling,
or the dwindling hum
of a struck gong,
dull vibrations,
barely audible.

An elegy.

Now I lay my heart to rest,
write an epilogical epitaph
to a series of failed
rose colored crushes.
I renounce limerence,
limbo,
a semicolon no longer
in wait for a complementary idea.

Perhaps my desolation
is the universe's design;
divine determination.
Always the diligent, conscientious
phantom,
I exist in pantomime -
the absence of words,
lack of punctuation,
rendering all meaningless,
mundane.

Quick -
      excite me!
Prove capital letters,
exclamation points,
have meaning;
no parentheses.

Let me share affirmations.
The prospect of being a point,
full stop,
final,

suggesting subsequent silence,
is unbearable.

No,
I am but the human question mark,
ever indicative of confusion,
unconditionally uncertain,
afraid there is no answer
to my query.

Prayer.

Alone again,
as always.
Please,
let me love ferociously
while I’m young.
Just once,
let my feelings not be precocious,
but grounded
in actions
rather
than daydreams.

Ashes.

As a mountain looms majestic over a
nameless tombstone;

As a river surges, waterfalls
cascading, the drips of a leaking
pipe inferior, inadequate;

As a roaring gust eclipses the
feeble breath of a dying animal,
runt of the litter;

I am *nothing* compared to you.

Save yourself.

Avert wallowing,
avoid addiction;
noxious adoration.

Believe,
find oxygen within yourself;
for you need no life mask
to inhale your own truth.

Moonrise.

After a plethora
of losses,
my heart tosses a rose,
a gosling in the moss,
growing, still innocent;
at what cost did I get here?

My naive honking is now
enlightened, enchanted -
dulcet, mellifluous music,
lilting;
let it transcend the earth,
scintillate another.

There is something
serendipitous
in my surreptitious wandering,
the waiting
I have had to endure;
but nothing is ever too late.

And as it turns out,
I was
a moiety, dichotomy
all this time.
I am not just a misfit,
a lone fowl,
but the moon;
mistaking my reflection
for inadequacy,
desiring the flawed perfection

of others.

Yet I need no nebula,
content to follow my own lunar
course,
no remorse,
a force to be reckoned with,
luminous in my own right.

For I am capable of
awakening
all kind of
nocturnal creatures.
Let the wolves howl,
as I bow out,
head emerging from under gossamer
wings.

So I fly,
breaking the sky's limit,
meeting myself in the stratosphere.
I shall orbit no longer,
but rather,
let the stars be attracted to me.

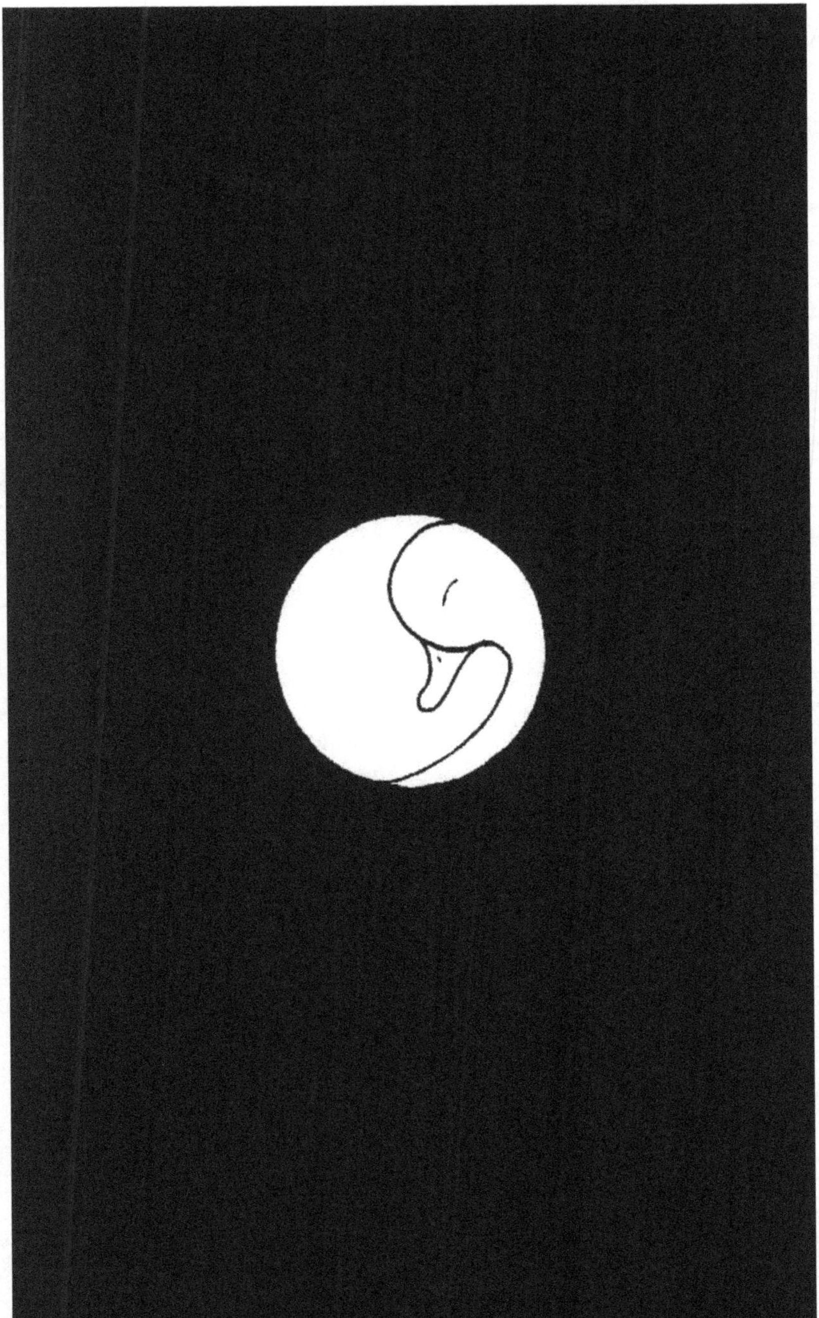

A note from the author:

Hello, hello, dear reader!

Thank you for reading my book - I hope you took away something, even if it's just that I write far too many nauseating love poems! Here's a bit about me:

There are many words or phrases I could use to describe myself, but I suppose "perpetually curious, enthusiastically eccentric violist and poet" probably fits best right now. I've lived in Brisbane, Australia all my life, but really do enjoy a frequent wander.

Creativity is my innate response to the world; I have to see my brain on paper to make sense of all I experience. Whether it be through music, art or poetry, I metaphorically meander through all the endeavours of my little rainbow heart, figure out my mental health struggles or simply appreciate a friend, always aiming to stretch my own limits. Because what could be better than trying to challenge societal expectations and quietly advocate for the introverted LGBTQ+ community?

So, no matter if I've casually sprung this book upon you or you've stumbled upon it in a moment of serendipity;

Here's to all the lonely, or anxious, or hurting hearts out there. I see you. Your stories deserve to be heard. Please don't give up just yet.

Once again, thank you for letting me take a little of your time. I truly, truly appreciate it.

Ash.

Ashleigh Abul is a violist, poet and general nonsense maker currently based in Brisbane, Australia.

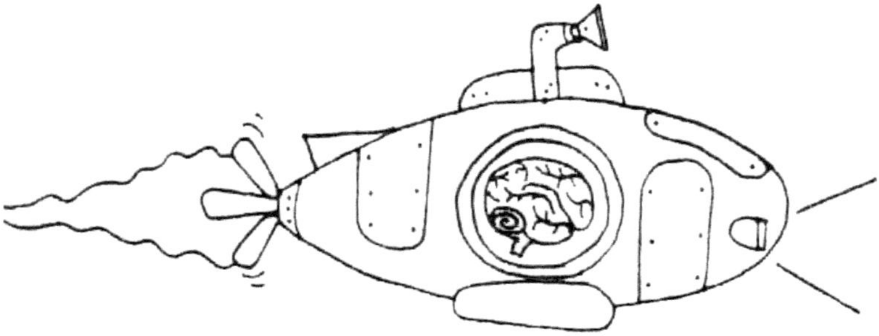

CPSIA information can be obtained
at www.ICGtesting.com
Printed in the USA
LVHW052352290719
625828LV00018B/1447/P

9 781723 466779